BEGINNING CLASSICAL GUITAR

A BEGINNER CLASSICAL GUITAR METHOD FOR ADULTS

DR. FRANCESCO BARONE

Beginning Classical Guitar

A Beginner Classical Guitar Method for Adults

Editors: Jonathan Rhodes Lee and Francesco Barone

Cover Design: germancreative

Formatting: HMD Publishing

Photography: Abigail O'Terry and Francesco Barone

ISBN: 979-8-9933042-0-5

First Printing, October 2025

Francesco Barone Publishing

15 Augustus Rd

Lexington, MA 02421

http://www.francescobaroneguitarstudio.com/

Roses are red,

Violets are blue,

I'm asking you,

Please leave a review.

Review now.

https://amzn.to/47bK5rr

Claim your FREE Video Files

Scan below to claim FREE video files that will accompany the exercises and tracks to this method.

These are not required to progress through the method,

but they will make it a lot easier...

...and they're FREE.

You can claim your FREE video files by scanning the QR code below.

Steps to open a QR code

1. Open the camera app.
2. Select the rear-facing camera in **Photo** mode.
3. Center the QR code you want to scan on the screen and hold your phone steady for a couple of seconds.
4. Tap the notification that pops up to open the link. (You will need to be connected to the internet to do this.)

CONTENTS

SECTION 2. BASIC NOTE READING

SECTION 3. INTRODUCTORY GUITAR SOLOS

Introduction

Over my nearly twenty years of teaching experience, I have found most classical guitar methods to be problematic for teenage and adult students. Traditional methods burden students with learning correct sitting position, left- and right-hand techniques, and basic reading skills all in the first lesson. Additionally, most traditional methods introduce students to folk songs and children's songs. These melodies have very little to do with the repertoire that inspired these students to take up classical guitar in the first place. The Suzuki method (a methodology that uses language acquisition skills to teach music to children) is a proven method for teaching children. However, the Suzuki method was not intended to teach beginner teenagers or adults. It delays music literacy skills far too long for students literate in their primary language, and it introduces new textures and techniques too slowly to engage more mature students.

The methodology used in this method is my own. It combines elements from the Suzuki, Traditional, and Provost methods (see "Classic Guitar Technique" in the bibliography). The first section introduces proper sitting position, basic left- and right-hand technique, and a few songs, which can be learned by rote memorization. This section most closely resembles the Suzuki method, and, like that method, includes "Twinkle Twinkle, Little Star." The second section most closely resembles the Traditional method, introducing basic reading skills. Unlike most traditional methods, I have worked to include excerpts from real repertoire, including music originally composed for classical guitar and broader classical repertoire. The third section introduces techniques to play multiple voices and introductory guitar solos. The sequencing of material in this section is informed by the Provost method.

The method is designed for the teenage and adult guitar student to gain a solid foundation in guitar fundamentals while being rewarded with noticeable progress and a quick path to learning and playing guitar solos. Although this method is intended for teenagers and adults, I have successfully used it for teaching students as young as ten years old.

Notation

Classical guitar music is notated in standard music notation, in which a five-bar staff represents the notes between lines and spaces. The symbol in front of each line is called the "treble clef" or "G clef." Famous acronyms for the note names on the treble clef are as follows: "Every Good Boy Does Fine" for the lines, and F-A-C-E (spelling the word "face") for the spaces (see Figure 1).

The entire gamut or register of the notes explored in this method are diagramed in Figure 2. At the start of each staff, the student will find a time signature (see Figure 3). In this book, we will deal with 4/4, 3/4, and 2/4 time; all this means is that each measure contains four, three, or two beats respectively. Each time signature is counted as follows: 1, 2, 3, 4 | 1, 2, 3, 4, etc. for 4/4 time, 1, 2, 3 | 1, 2, 3, etc. for 3/4 time, and 1, 2 | 1, 2, etc. for 2/4 time. The type of note head and stem (if applicable) notate the rhythm, along with their parallel rests or measured silence. Note that beats can be subdivided, as shown in Figure 4. Figure 5 shows the same rhythmic breakdown by measure, but in this case, it shows rests; these notations indicate silences that occur for the length of time indicated (one-third beat, one-half beat, one beat, two beats, etc.).

Figure 1

Figure 2

Figure 3

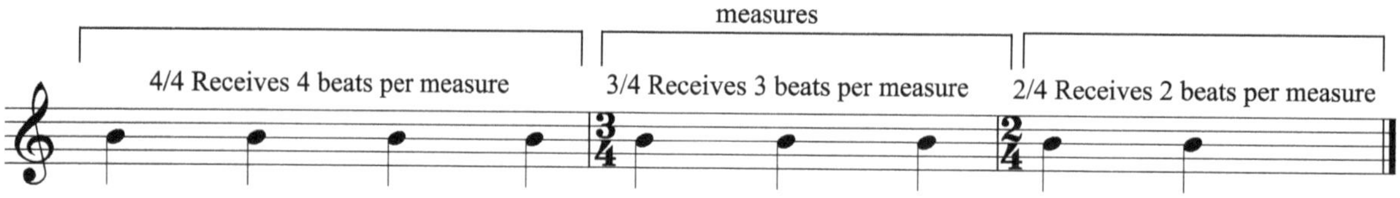

Figure 4

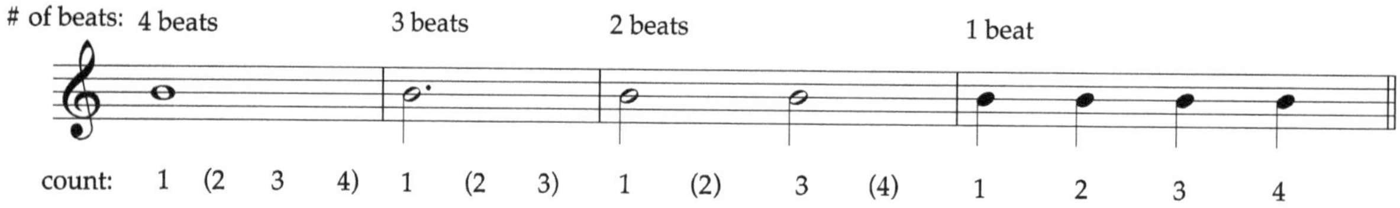

Figure 5

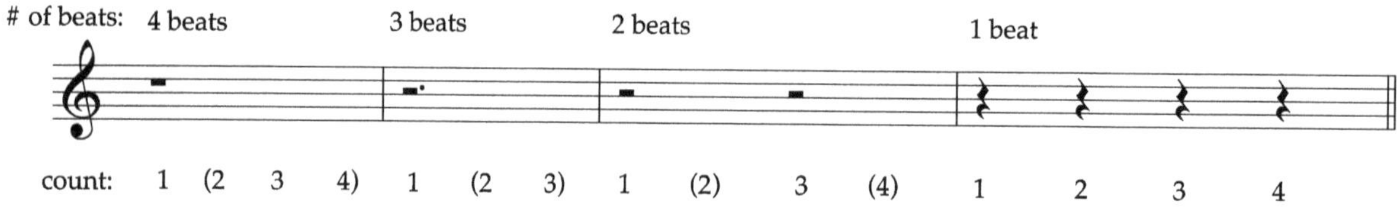

There is specific notation for labeling the right- and left-hand fingers within a score. The right-hand fingers are labeled in the following manner: thumb (p), index (i), middle (m), ring (a), and pinky (c). The left-hand fingers are labeled in the following manner: index (1), middle (2), ring (3), and pinky (4). Zero (0) represents an open string (see Figure 6). These designations are standard for notating and discussing the left-hand fingers. Figure 7 displays left- and right-hand fingerings notated in a musical excerpt.

Figure 6

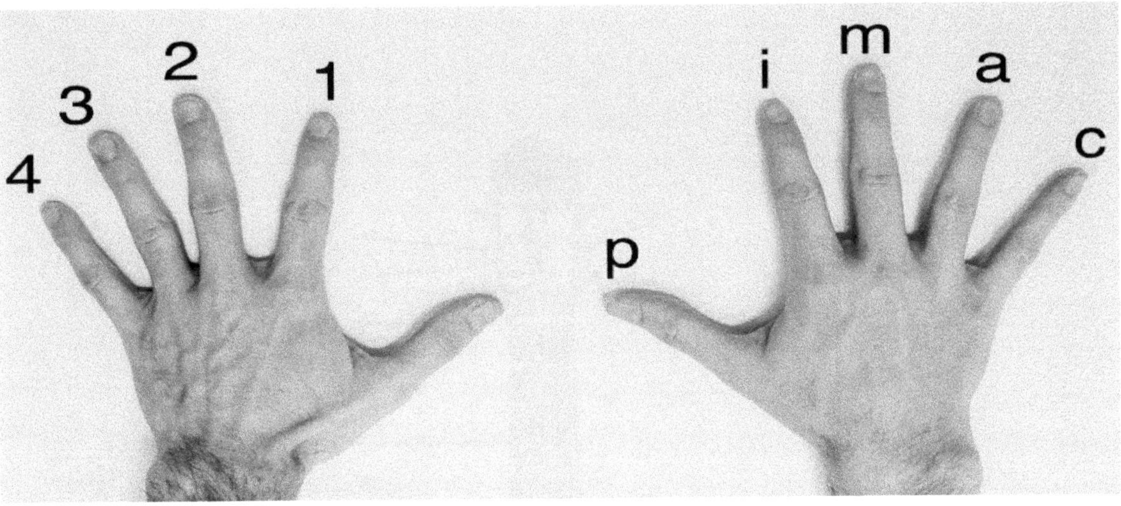

Figure 7

The strings are labeled one through six, beginning with the thinnest string. A specific string is indicated in the score by a marking including the string number circled; the first (highest-pitched) string would be shown as follows: ①.

In the first section, this method will use a system called "tablature" to notate exact pitches, headed "TAB" at the beginning of a six-line staff, as shown in Figure 8. Each of these lines represents a string on the guitar, oriented with the guitar's highest-pitched (first) string on the top of the TAB staff and the guitar's lowest (sixth) string at the bottom. Numbers on each represented string represent frets. "0" means to play the string open; "1" means to press the first fret; "2" means to press the second fret; "3" means to press the third fret; and so on.

Figure 8

Parts of the Guitar

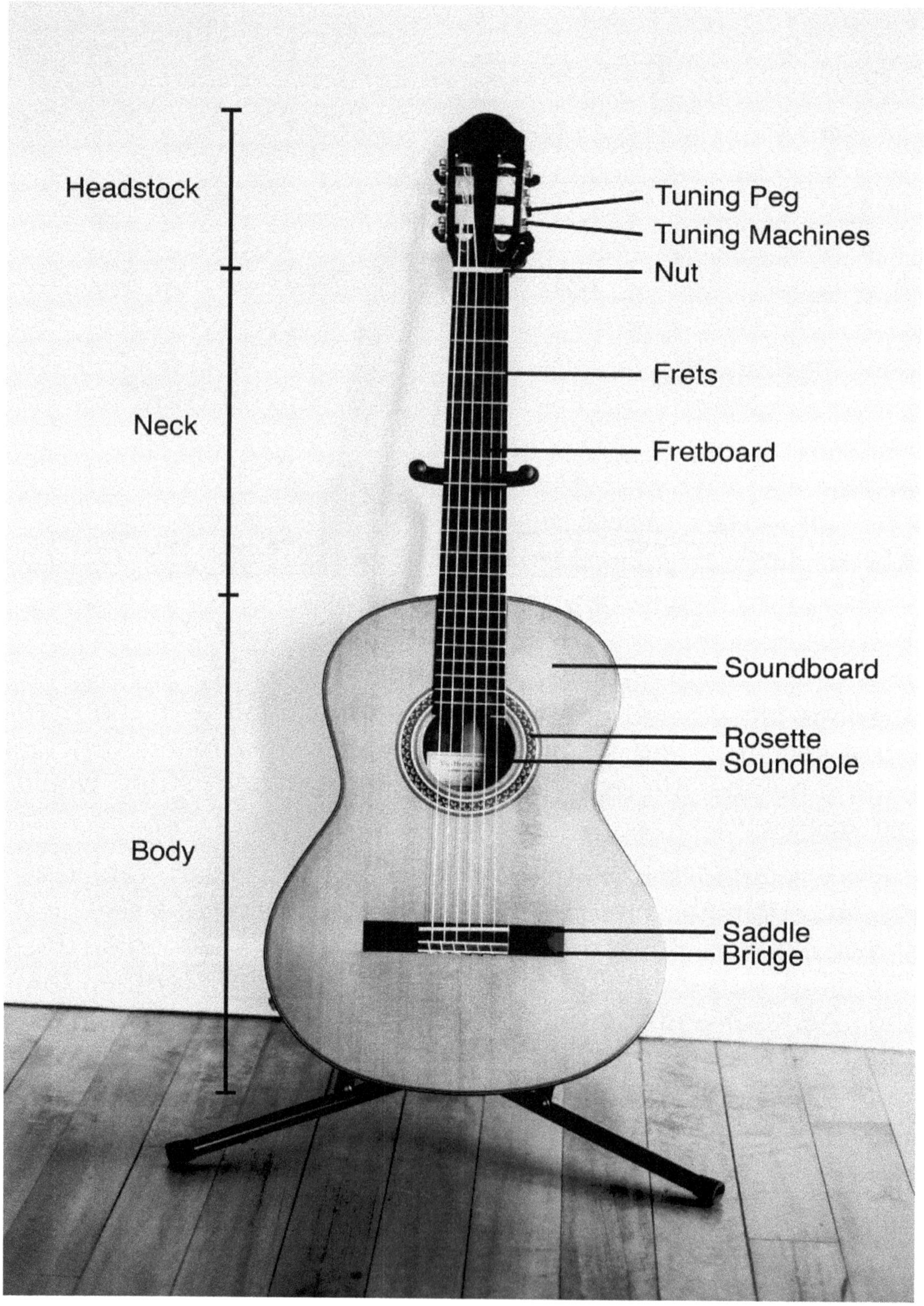

Joints of the Right Hand

This method will frequently refer to the various joints of the right hand, which are labeled in the diagram below. The joints that are labeled on the i finger also apply to the related joints of the m, a, and c fingers.

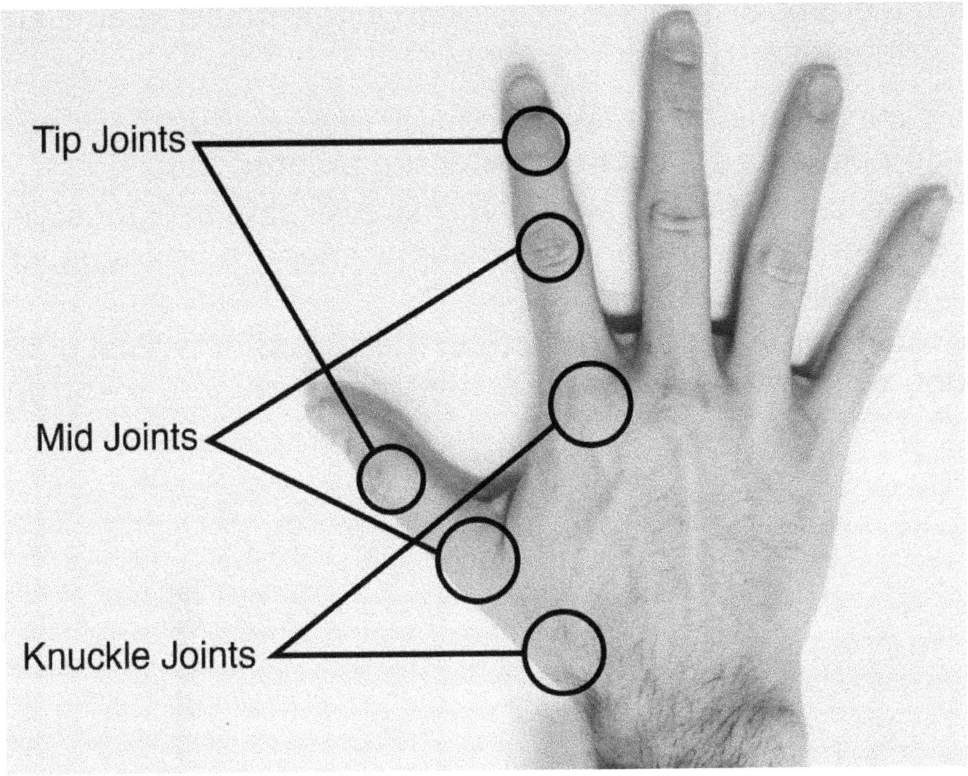

Materials

Undertaking guitar study will not require an unreasonably large investment of money. The primary materials you will need are listed below:

- Classical Guitar
- Footstool
- Tuner

Additional materials will be needed once you begin nail playing; these are listed below:

- Nail File
- Buffer

Each of the necessary materials will be described in more detail below.

Classical Guitar

The most essential purchase to study guitar is a classical guitar. The following features distinguish a classical guitar (below image left) from a steel string guitar (below image right).

- The tuning pegs of a classical guitar are pointed back while the tuning pegs of a steel string guitar are pointed out.
- The classical guitar has a relatively smaller figure-eight style body, in contrast to the larger dreadnaught shape of many steel string acoustic guitars.
- The most notable difference lies in the strings. Classical guitars are strung with nylon strings, while steel strings guitars are strung with steel (as the name suggests).

Cordoba is a factory manufacturer that produces fine instruments at low price points. Kenny Hill guitars are semi-handmade and are wonderful high-end student guitars for more serious players. Here is a list of various student instruments at different price points that I would recommend:

$100- 200: Cordoba C1M

$300- 400: Cordoba C5

$500- 600: Cordoba C7

$700- 1000: Hill New World Estudio

$1000- 2500: Hill New World Player with Raised Fingerboard

Footstool

A footstool is a device that elevates the left leg while the guitar is being held. Various other guitar supports can be used instead of the footstool, although I would recommend the latter to begin. For those who prefer a support, I use and would recommend a Sagework guitar support.

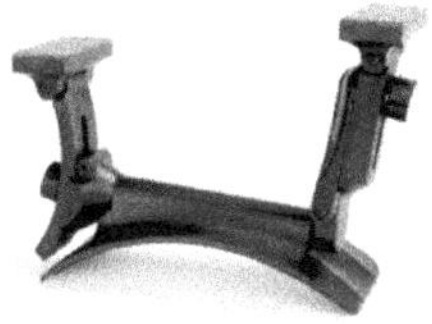

Tuner

The most affordable and intuitive solution for tuning the guitar is the GuitarTuna app.

Headstock guitar tuners are nice for ease and concealment while tuning onstage. The one listed is the tuner I personally use and recommend to my students.

Nail File

You will need a nail file to adjust the length and shape of the nails on the right hand. I recommend a glass nail file, although a steel diamond nail file or emery board will work as well.

Buffer

A nail buffer will smooth the edge of the right-hand nails after they are filed. I recommend using 500 grit open coat sandpaper, although an emery board or nail buffer will work as well.

You can pick up everything right here!

Section I:

Learning by Rote

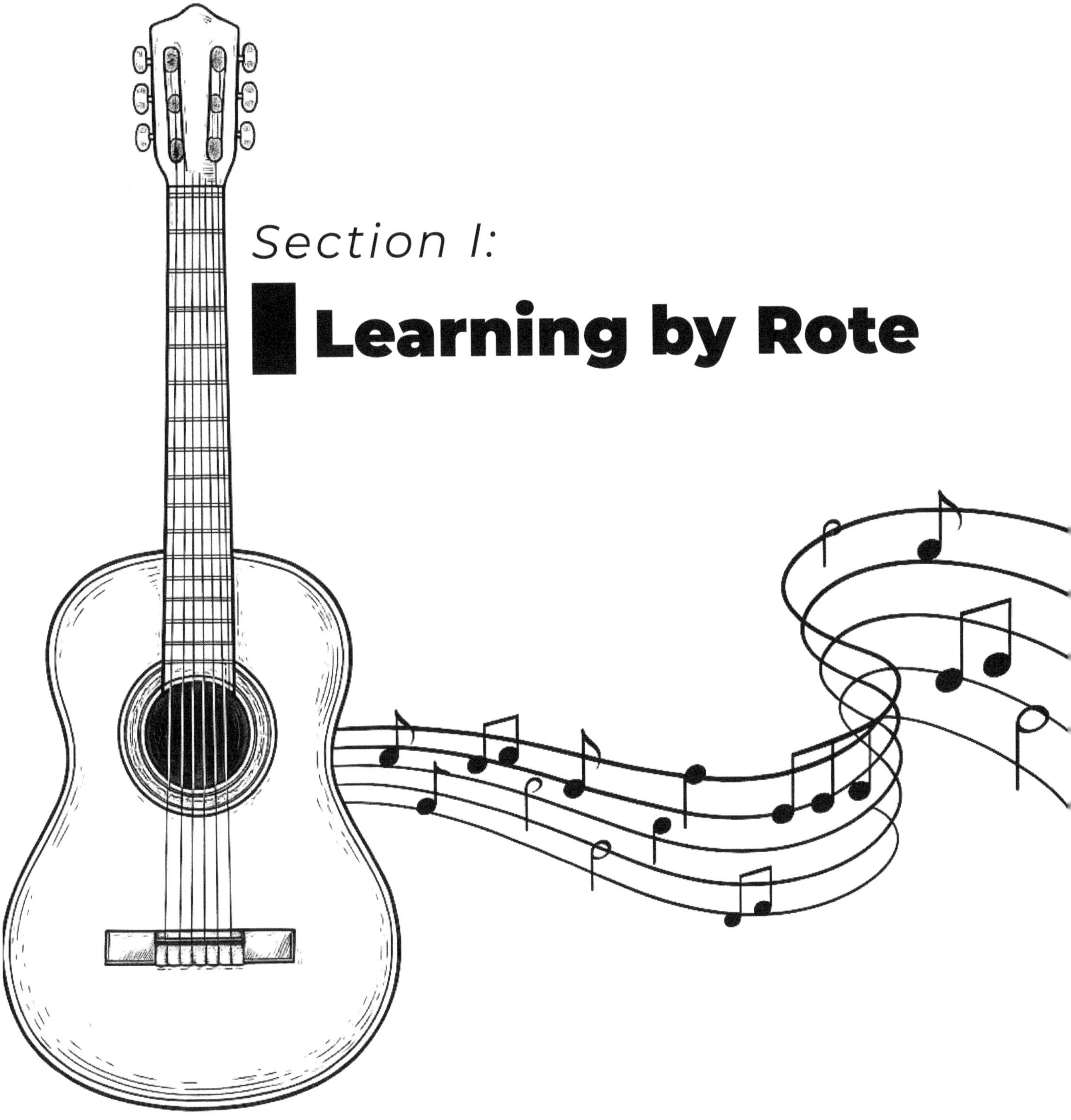

Throughout this section, you will learn by watching and listening. Accompaniment videos or a demonstration from your instructor will be critical in learning these pieces. The purpose of the notation in this section is to assist you in most quickly learning the exercises and pieces. Each pitch is notated in three ways: 1) note names written above, 2) pitches written in standard music notation, and 3) pitches notated in TAB (see the example below). The purpose of this section is to develop foundational habits including proper sitting position, right- and left-hand technique, and the ability to play a few introductory melodies with ease.

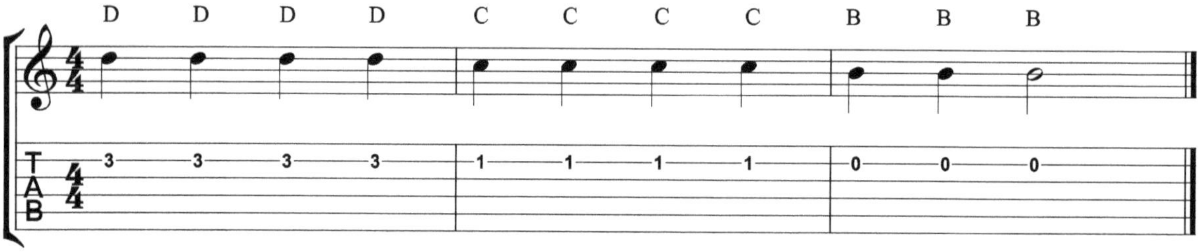

• SITTING AND HOLDING THE GUITAR

Use the following steps to set up a proper sitting position.

1. Establish the correct height of the footstool or guitar support.
2. Sit straight and on the front edge of the chair. Keep your shoulders lowered and even.
3. Your right foot should be flat on the floor and at roughly a 45-degree angle. The heel should be positioned underneath the kneecap.
4. The curve of the guitar body should rest on the left side of your lap.
5. The side of the body of the guitar should rest on your inner right thigh.
6. The sixth tuning peg of guitar should roughly be at or above eye level.
7. The neck of the guitar should be slightly forward to the plane of your body.
8. The body of the guitar should be tilted slightly toward the ceiling.
9. Both shoulders should be relaxed and level.

ESTABLISHING THE RIGHT-HAND POSITION

Use the following steps to set up the right hand.

1. The forearm should rest approximately one to two inches from the elbow on top of the guitar. Position the forearm over the bridge.

2. Position the forearm over the strings and make a thumbs up.

3. Relax the wrist and place the thumb on the fourth string (thinnest wound string). Observe the angle of the wrist.

4. With the thumb on the fourth string, allow the fingers to open.

5. If necessary, rotate the wrist to achieve proper alignment.

• LEARNING REST STROKES

Rest strokes are a technique where the finger plays a string and then comes to rest on the next lowest string. Use the following steps to execute alternating rest strokes between the (i) and (m) fingers.

1. Place the middle finger (m) on the first string ①.

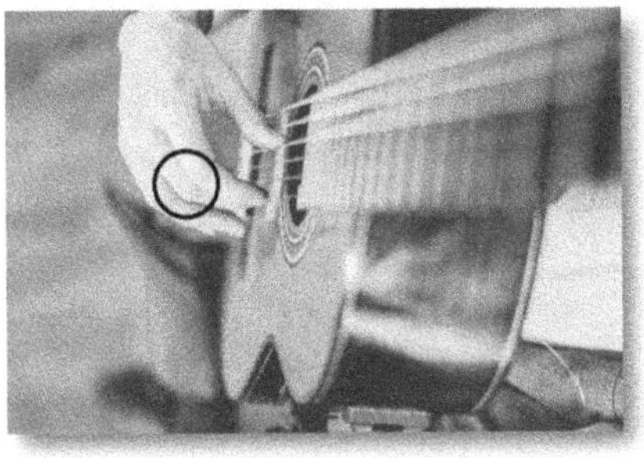

2. Position the finger mid-knuckle over the string to be plucked.

3. Pluck the string by pushing the finger through the string (the motion should come from the knuckle joint). Rest on the next string (string 2). Bring the next finger (i) to pluck into position.

4. When m plays, always move the "a" and pinky with it.

• LEFT HAND POSITION/ LEARNING D, C, & B

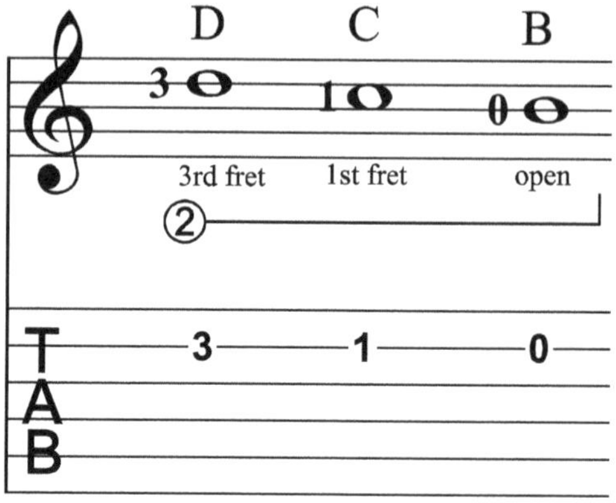

Use the following steps to set up the left hand.

1. Allow your left hand to hang by your side. Your palm should be turned face up.

2. From the elbow, lift your forearm until your fingers are in front of the guitar neck and your thumb is behind it.

3. Place your fingers on the second string, lining up with corresponding frets. Place the thumb behind the neck roughly behind the middle finger.

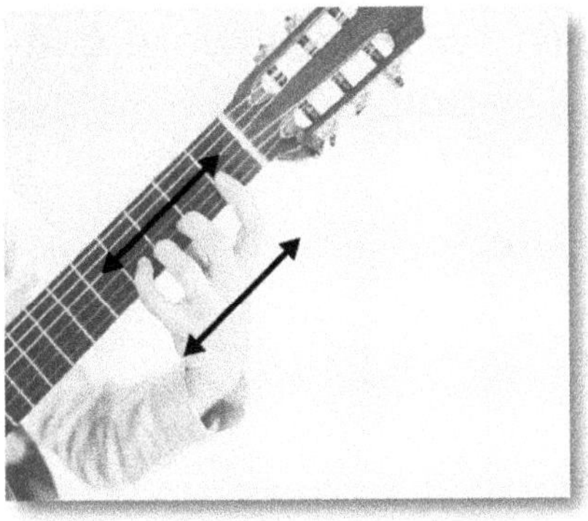

4. Make sure that your knuckles are parallel to the neck.

5. Place your third finger on its tip, and snug next to the third fret. If your finger is on top of the fret, it will thud; if it is too far away, it will buzz.

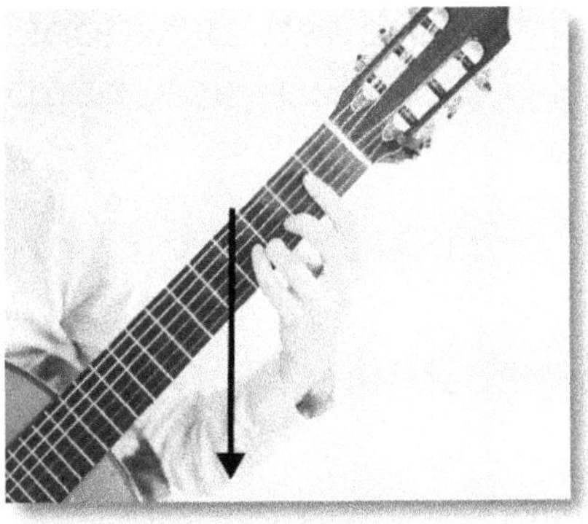

6. Feel the weight of the arm (hanging from your elbow) depressing the note. Play the note with the right hand. If the last two steps were executed correctly, a D should sound.

7. Reach back with the first finger and place it snug next to the first fret of the second strings. The finger should be placed flat and on the left side.

8. Lift the third finger. Play the note with the right hand. If the last two steps were executed correctly, a C should sound.

9. Allow the first and third fingers to hover over the neck. Play the note on the second string unfretted. You have just played a B!

D, C, B Exercise

Now that you have learned a proper sitting, right and left positions, and your first notes, you are ready to learn the D, C, B Exercise. Keep the following in mind while playing the exercise.

- Make sure you have established a proper sitting position, right-hand position, and left-hand position.
- Make sure you are playing the exercise with rest strokes. The thumb should be rested on the fourth string.
- Make sure that the third finger is played curled and on the tip. The first finger should be played flat and on the left side.

D, C, B Exercise

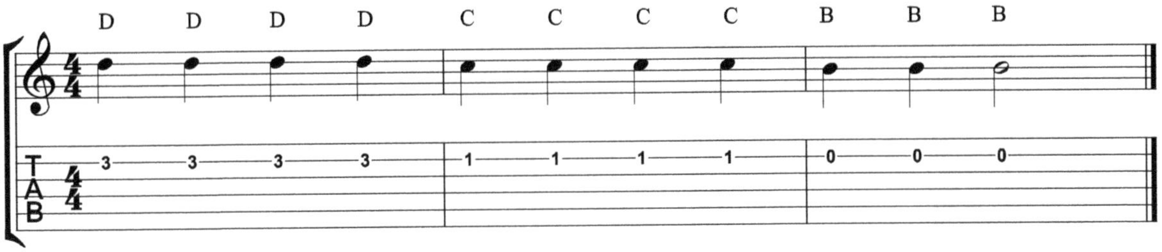

El Matador
Francisco Baron (b. 1986)

Now we are ready to apply what we have learned to a melody. "El Matador" is a melody in Phrygian mode that is intended to evoke the music associated with Spanish bullfighting. Give this piece the same consideration that you gave to the previous exercise. You should also apply the same bullet points that you applied in the last exercise to this piece.

El Matador

• RIGHT-HAND SHIFTING

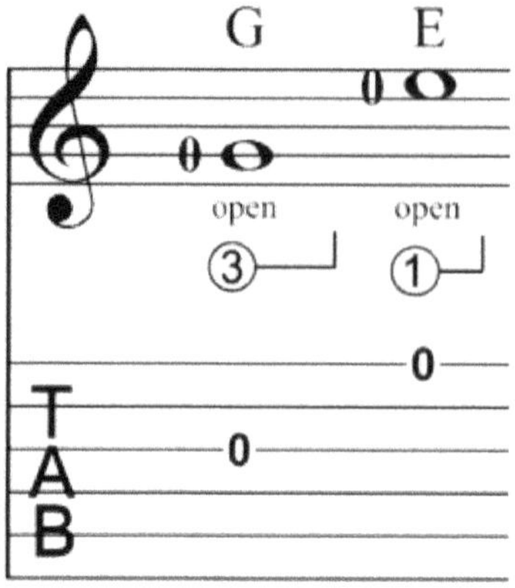

Up to this point we have been playing on a single string with the thumb rested on the fourth string. Right-hand shifting will allow us to move between strings. New notes on the third (G) and first (E) strings are notated. Thumb placement is marked with an x in both standard notation and tablature. Step-by-step instructions will be given for the next exercise.

1. Establish the right-hand position on the third string with the thumb placed on the fifth string and mid-joint over the third string (see image below).
2. Pluck the first two notes beginning with the i finger, then STOP at the double bar line.
3. Lift the right arm slightly so that the weight of the arm is off the guitar and slide until the thumb is rested on the fourth string and the mid-joints are over the second string (see the image below).
4. Pluck the second two notes beginning with the i finger, then STOP at the double bar line.
5. Lift the right arm slightly so that the weight of the arm is off the guitar and slide until the thumb is rested on the third string and the mid-joints are over the first string (see image below).
6. Pluck the next two notes beginning with the i finger, then STOP at the double bar line.

7. Lift the right arm slightly so that the weight of the arm is off the guitar and slide until the thumb is rested on the fourth string and the mid-joints are over the second string (see image below).
8. Play the final note.

Once you have practiced the piece this way and sliding is comfortable between strings, try playing the exercise without observing the double bar lines.

Shifting Exercise

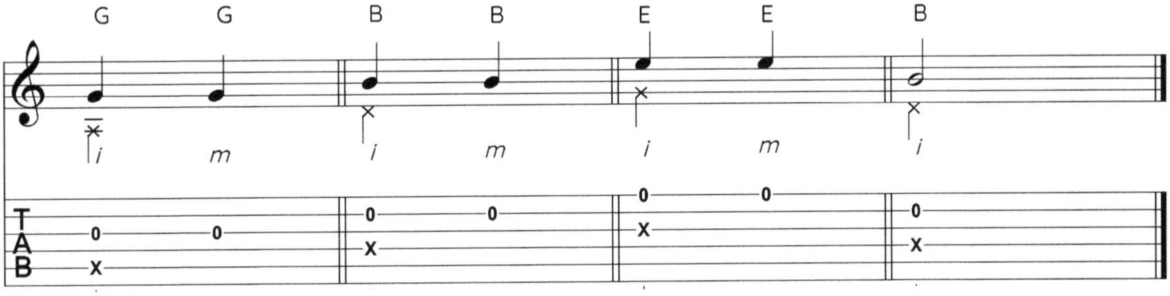

• NOTES ON THE THIRD STRING/G PENTACHORD

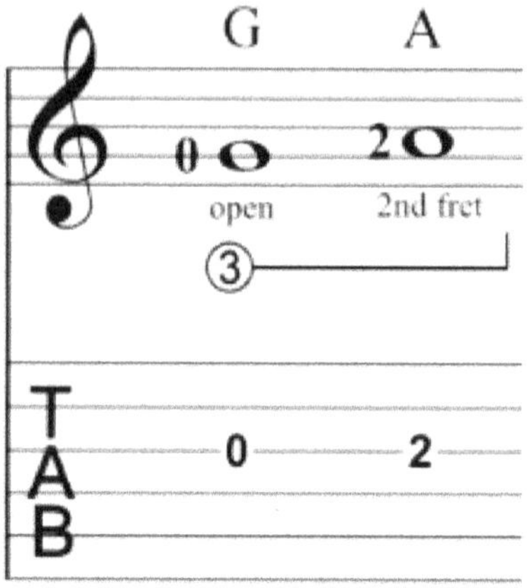

In addition to the G note that we have previously learned, we will now be learning the A note, which is on the second fret of the same string. The G pentachord will introduce these new notes. Consider the following while learning the G pentachord.

- Give attention to the right-hand shifting. I would begin by pausing at the double bar lines as in the previous exercise. Also, be aware of the right-hand fingering.
- Make sure notes A and D are being played with the left-hand fingers curled and on their tips. The C note should be played flat and on its left side.
- Say the note names out loud while playing in order to develop familiarity with the location of each note on the fretboard.

G Pentachord

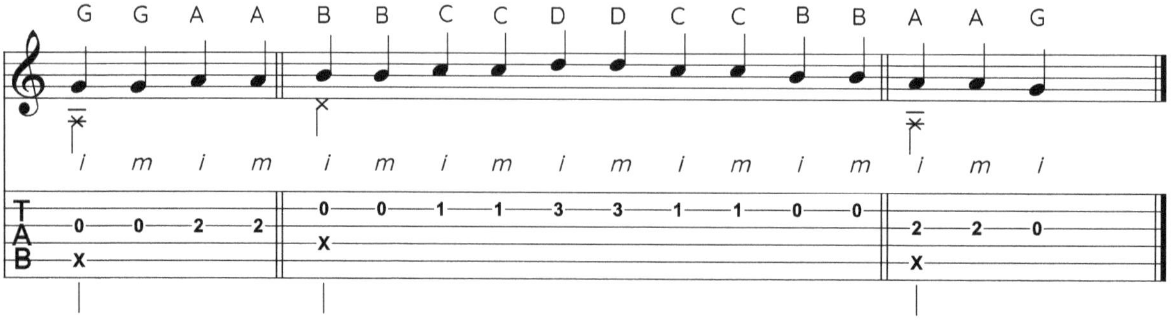

Twinkle, Twinkle, Little Star
Traditional

"Twinkle, Twinkle, Little Star" combines all the techniques, notes, and materials learned thus far. You want to make sure to play it with proper technique. As you practice, you will note one new feature: the repeated i between every two measures. This fingering allows for more fluid phrasing and continuity throughout the piece. Observe the following while playing:

- Make sure to observe proper right-hand shifting and fingerings.
- Make sure notes A and D are being played with the left-hand fingers curled and on their tips. The C note should be played flat and on its left side.
- Say the note names out loud while playing in order to develop familiarity with the location of each note on the fretboard.

Twinkle, Twinkle, Little Star

• NAILS

In what follows, I offer general guidelines to provide students with a starting place for filing their nails. Note, however, that every hand is different, and exact procedures will vary depending on the physiology of each hand.

Note to the Teacher

Although I placed this topic at the end of Section I, it can be introduced as soon as the first lesson and as late as the introduction of the C scale. However, the student will need to be comfortable with nail playing upon entering Section III of this method.

File fingers p, i, m and a with the following steps.

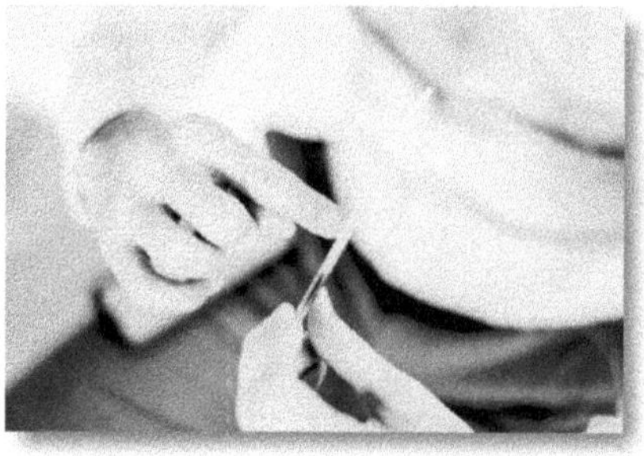

1. Place the file perpendicular to the nail at a 45-degree angle. This stroke will shorten the length of the nail.

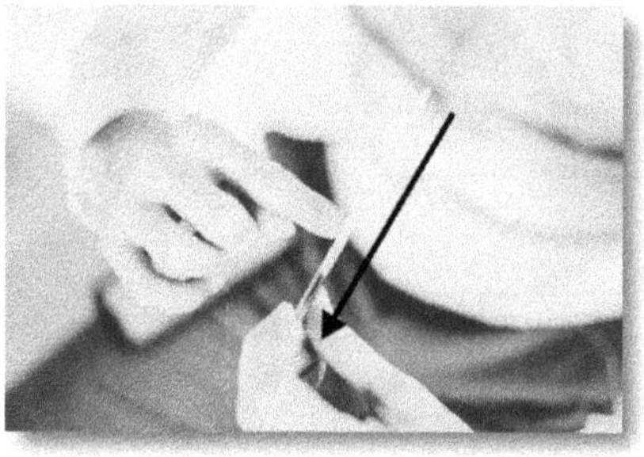

2. Swipe in one direction.

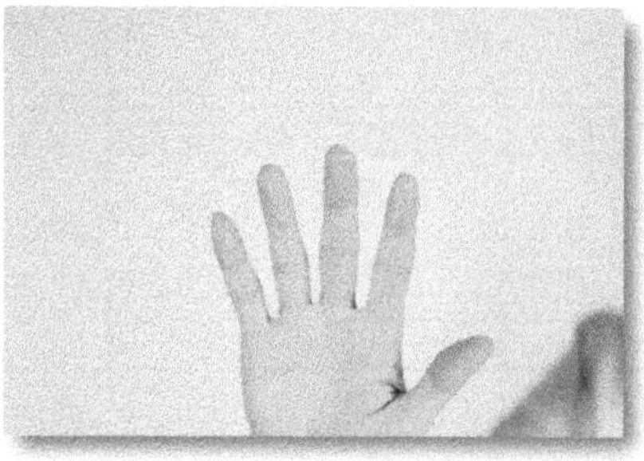

3. The nail should just peek over the finger when the palm is facing you. Swiping in one direction produces a smoother edge and prevents damage to the nail grain. File until the desired length is achieved.

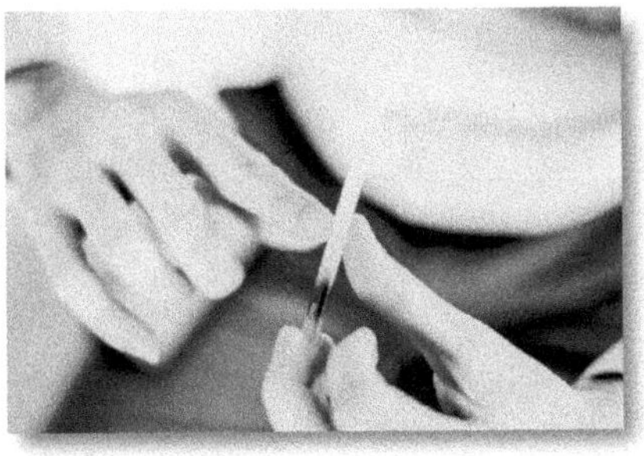

4. Place the file on the left nail/finger interface (where the left edge of the nail meets the flesh of the finger) and angle it to create a ramp that covers about 75% of the nail. This stroke will create the ramp in which the nail will glide over the string. The file should be placed at a 45-degree angle.

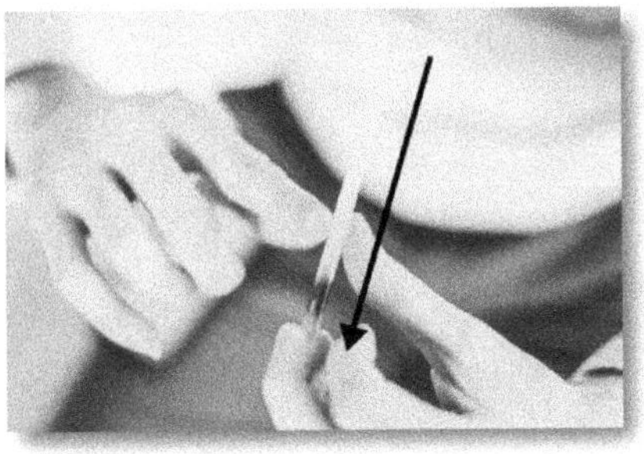

5. Swipe in one direction. Until the desired length is achieved.

6. Use a buffer to smooth the edge of the nail. The buffer should be angled at a 90-degree angle and can be used in both directions.

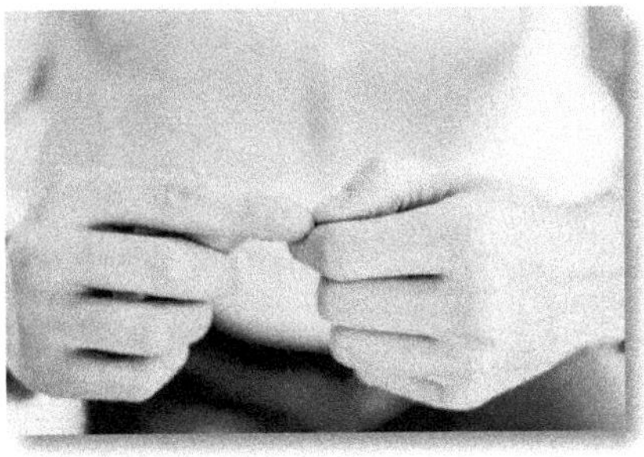

7. Once finished, use the edge of another nail to check the smoothness. The newly buffed nail should feel smooth like a mirror.

8. Play a string with the newly filed nail. If there is resistance, it is likely that the corner of the nail needs to be swiped once or twice more.

Section II:

Basic Note Reading

The purpose of the following section is to develop basic note reading skills. Standard notation will be exclusively used with left-hand fingerings given for new notes as a learning aid (see the below figure). You should assume that right-hand fingerings will alternate. Right-hand fingerings will be given for any divergence from a typical i-m or m-i pattern. In this section, the student will learn the notes in the first position as well, as basic rhythmic notation. I have selected mostly classical melodies as examples, augmented by the occasional traditional folk song or children's song.

• NOTES ON THE TOP THREE STRINGS

Notes on the Second and Third Strings

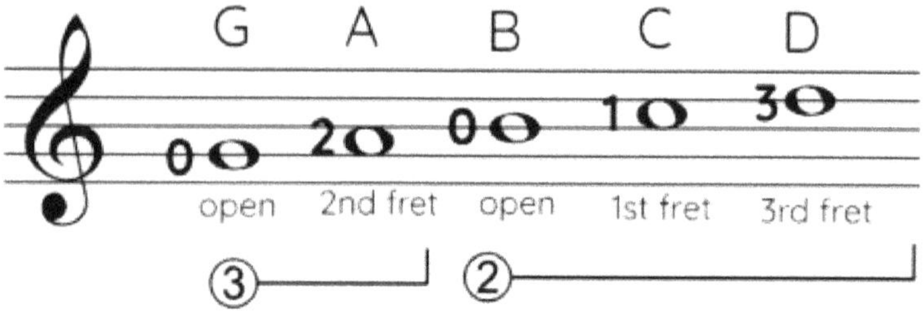

Basic Rhythms

Basic rhythms and their corresponding rests have been presented in the introduction of this method and include quarter, half, dotted half and whole notes. Below are exercises useful for practicing these rhythms. The below exercises as well as rhythmic exercises to follow are intended to be clapped rather than played. I notated each rhythm with a consistent B simply for visual clarity.

Rhythmic Exercise 1

Rhythmic Exercise 2

Rhythmic Exercise 3

Lightly Row
Traditional

"Lightly Row" incorporates no new skills or notes other than that it is notated in standard notation. It provides a seamless segue into reading notes.

- Before attempting to play, clap the rhythms giving each of the quarter notes one beat and half notes two beats. Once work begins on the guitar, say the note names and rhythms out loud while playing.
- Note the repeated i fingerings between measures 4 and 5 and 8 and 9.
- Don't forget to play with a strong sitting position, left-hand position, and right-hand position.

Lightly Row

Notes on the First String

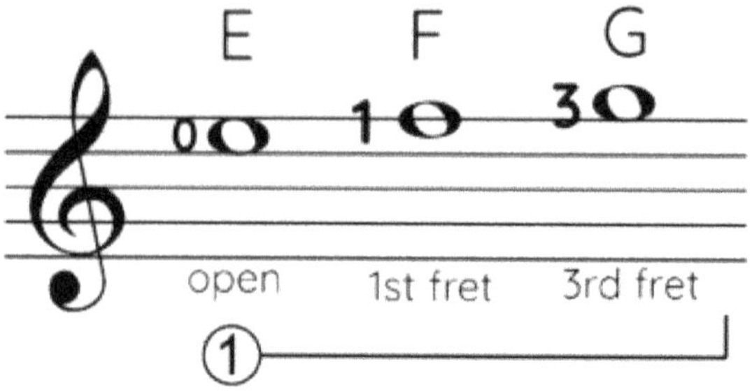

We Three Kings
Traditional

"We Three Kings" is a Christmas carol that incorporates new notes on the first string. This is the first piece in 3/4 included in this section. Make sure to count each measure to three as well as observe the dotted half notes which are three beats. The final two notes form a descending inverted cross, which is a right-hand shift that contrasts the natural lay of the hand (for example, using the i finger to play the first string followed by the m finger to play the second). To compensate, make sure that you are intentionally sliding the forearm.

- Count out loud and be aware of the new rhythmic elements in 3/4.
- Be aware of the final two notes of the piece, which form an inverted descending cross.
- Continue to be aware of the technical consideration observed in the previous exercises.
- Continue to say note names out loud while playing.

We Three Kings

Supplemental: Lesson in C
op. 31, no. 13
Fernando Sor (1778–1839)

The supplemental material here and elsewhere throughout the book can be used to further reinforce newly introduced concepts, serve as reading material, or be skipped over. These selections can also make good recital pieces, since they are generally longer and are full-length pieces rather than excerpts.

Spanish guitar composer Fernando Sor was one of the most influential guitar composers of the classical period. In addition to writing concert music for the guitar including sonatas and theme and variations, Sor wrote numerous volumes of etudes. This excerpt includes a simplified version of the introductory melody from op. 31, no. 13.

- Note the repeated m fingers between phrases.
- Note the inverted crosses in lines 2 and 4.
- Continue to sing note names out loud, count and consider technical points.

Lesson in C

• PICKUP NOTES & TIES

Pickup Notes

A pickup note is an incomplete measure that leads to the downbeat. The pickup is counted as the final beat (or beats) leading into the opening measure. The final measure compensates for the missing beats in the pickup; thus, the pickup plus the final measure always equals a full measure. The rhythmic exercises below show the proper count for each pickup.

Rhythmic Exercise 4

Rhythmic Exercise 5

Rhythmic Exercise 6

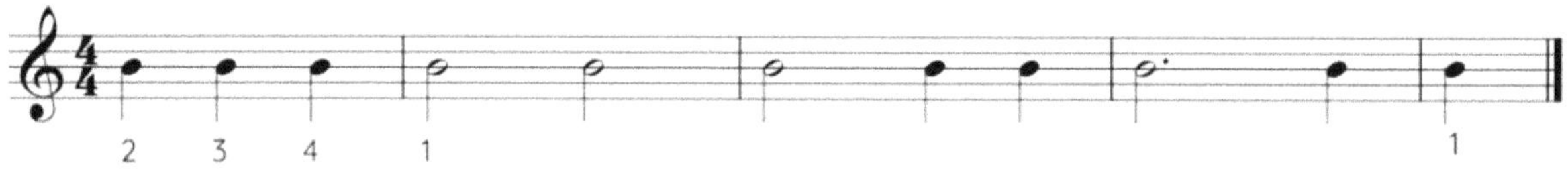

Blue Bells of Scotland
Dora Jordan (1761–1816)

"Blue Bells of Scotland" is a Scottish folksong composed by Dorothea ("Dora") Jordan. Joseph Haydn composed an arrangement of this tune for violin, cello, and keyboard (Hob. 31a: 176). I displaced the latter half of the melody by one octave for the purposes of this method.

⅄ Count the opening pickup as beat 4.

- Be aware of the inverted cross between F and D at the end of each line.
- Continue to sing note names, count, and be aware of sitting position and hand position.

Blue Bells of Scotland

Supplemental: O Splendor of God's Glory Bright
John D. Brunk (1872–1926)

"O Splendor of God's Glory Bright" is a church hymn with text originating from Ambrose of Milan. The text was set to this melody by John D. Brunk (1872–1926), a Mennonite residing in the United States during the nineteenth century.

I have included all of the right-hand fingerings because of the inverted descending string cross in the beginning of the piece, which might confuse some players. I also displaced the A and G notes in the last line by one octave for the purposes of this method.

- Make sure to count the rhythm out loud considering the quarter note pickup.
- Note the descending inverted crosses in mm. 1 and 10 as well as the repeated i fingerings between phrases.
- Continuing saying note names out loud as well as being aware of technical considerations.

O Splendor of God's Glory Bright

Ties

A tie joins two notes across a bar line, thus it is counted as one long note. The proper count for a tied note is articulated in the below exercise.

Rhythmic Exercise 7

Plaisir d'amour
Jean-Paul-Égide Martini (1872–1926)

"Plaisir d'amour" [Pleasure of Love] is a French song composed by Jean-Paul-Égide Martini (1741–1816). It was arranged for orchestra by romantic composer and guitarist Hector Berlioz in 1859 (cataloged as H134). This piece introduces use of the tie.

- Make sure to count the rhythm out loud considering the quarter note pickup as well as the tied notes.
- Observe the double i finger in the middle of the second line.
- Continuing saying note names out loud as well as being aware of technical considerations.

Plaisir d'amour

Supplemental: Far, Far beyond the Starry Sky
Carl Plank (1801-1825)

"Far, Far beyond the Starry Sky" is authored by Karl Plank and set to an old English tune. It can serve as supplemental material for tied notes as well as additional reading material.

- Observe the tied notes.
- Observe the inverted crosses in mm. 6, 14, 23 and 30 as well as the repeated fingers between phrases.
- Continuing saying note names out loud as well as being aware of technical considerations.

Far, Far beyond the Starry Sky

When the Saints Go Marching In
Traditional

"When the Saints Go Marching In" serves as a great review for pickups and tied notes. The pickup consists of three notes which begin on beat 2. It is the most rhythmically complex piece introduced thus far.

- Count out loud the piece while observing the pickup notes and ties.
- Be aware of the repeated m and i fingers on the second line.
- Continue to sing note names out loud and consider technical points.

When the Saints Go Marching In

• EIGHTH NOTES & DOTTED QUARTER NOTES

Eighth Notes

Thus far, the smallest note duration we have played is the quarter note, a one-beat note. The eighth note is the first subdivision that will be introduced. An eighth note sustains for one half beat, the "offbeat," and is counted with the word "and" (&). Two eighth notes can fit into the space of one quarter note. The example below will clarify the relationship between quarter and half notes. Make sure to follow the count notated below.

Rhythmic Exercise 8

L'Éléphant
From Le Carnaval des animaux
Camille Saint-Saëns (1835–1921)

"L'Éléphant" [The Elephant] is the first of three melodies from Camille Saint-Saëns's *Le Carnaval des animaux* [The Carnival of the Animals] included in this method. This excerpt was transposed as well as changed from 3/8 to 3/4.

- Make sure to count out loud away from the guitar and while playing, giving special consideration to the eighth notes.
- Note the inverted descending string cross between mm. 5-6 and mm. 6-7.
- Continue to sing note names out loud and consider technical points.

L'Éléphant

Supplemental: In Days of Old
English folk melody

In Days of Old is a hymn authored by John D. Martin set to an English traditional melody. This melody was arranged as a hymn by 20th century English composer Ralph Vaughn Williams. The selection was also transposed and melody slightly changed for pedagogical considerations.

- Make sure to count out loud away from the guitar and while playing.
- Note the few left hand finger doublings.
- Continue to sing note names out loud.

In Days of Old

Dotted Quarter Notes

A dotted quarter note sustains for one-and-a-half beats. A dot next to a note adds one half of the preceding note's value; for instance, a dotted half note sustains for three beats, since the half note equals two beats and the dot equals one beat (half of the half note's value). The same is true for a dotted quarter note; the dot would add a half beat to the quarter note, since the quarter note is equal to one beat, and the dot receives half of that note's value.

Rhythmic Exercise 9

Repeat Bar Lines

Repeat bar lines indicate that a selection of music should be repeated. An end repeat (see images below) signals that the music preceding it should be repeated. A start repeat indicates the beginning of the repeated section. If there is no Start repeat before an End repeat it is understood that the repeated section begins at the beginning of the piece. In the below example, the music in-between the repeat bar lines should be repeated.

End Repeat

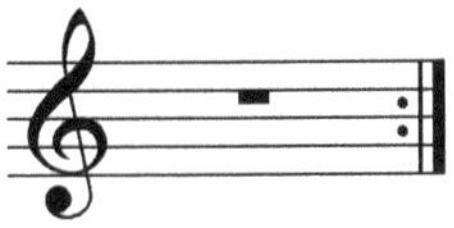

Start Repeat

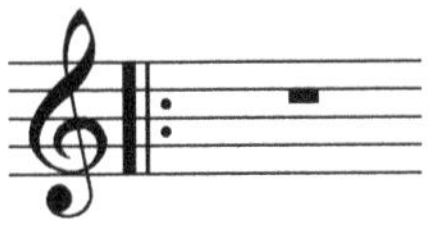

Example Utilizing End & Start Repeats

An die Freude
From Symphony no. 9 in D minor, op. 125
Ludwig van Beethoven (1770–1827)

"An die Freude" [Ode to Joy] was the final choral melody of Beethoven's monumental ninth symphony, op. 125. The melody introduces the dotted quarter note as well as repeat bar lines. The key has been changed from the original, D major to C major for ease of reading.

- Make sure to count out loud away from the guitar and while playing, giving special consideration to the newly introduced dotted-quarter note rhythm and repeat bar line.
- Note the repeated m fingers throughout the melody.
- Continue to sing note names out loud and consider technical points.

An die Freude

Supplemental: Some Sweet Day When Life is Over
S.H. Chord (fl. 1892)

"Some Sweet Day When Life is Over" (also known as "Some Sweet Day") is a church hymn composed by S. H. Chord.

- Make sure to count out loud away from the guitar and while playing, giving special consideration to the newly introduced dotted-quarter note rhythm.
- Note the inverted crosses and double m finger between mm. 14- 15.
- Continue to sing note names out loud and consider technical points.

Some Sweet Day When Life is Over

• NOTES ON THE FOURTH STRING + C

The C-major scale includes the introduced notes as well as all the others studied up to this point. Rest the thumb on the sixth string (marked with an x note head) while playing the new notes on the fourth and fifth strings. Thumb movement for the remainder of the scale will be the same as the G Pentachord introduced in Section I.

C-Major Scale

Free Strokes

An alternative to a rest stroke, free strokes are characteristically lighter and less full than rest strokes. They also allow the player to execute multiple notes at the same time (explained further later in this method). The steps for playing free strokes are listed below.

1. Position the fingers as if to play rest strokes on the first string with the mid-joint over the first string.

2. Slide the forearm forward until the knuckle joint is over the first string (Unlike the rest stroke, in this stroke, the knuckle joint should be over the string that you are playing).

3. Pluck the string with the i finger from the knuckle joint. Rather than landing on the second string, the finger will clear the lower strings and follow-through into the palm of the hand.

4. Allow the m finger to fall to the first string. Keep i in the hand.

5. Play the m finger allowing the finger to follow-through into the palm of the hand. The i finger will return to the string.

6. Repeat steps 3-5.

You should practice this exercise until you can execute free strokes comfortably. Once this is achieved, practice the D, C, B exercise and El Matador that you learned in Section I with free strokes. Once these can be comfortably played, begin practicing the C-major scale with free strokes in addition to rest strokes. Once you are comfortable playing the C scale with free strokes, I would learn any new pieces in Section II with rest strokes and free strokes.

Marche royale du lion
From Le Carnival des animaux
Camille Saint-Saëns (1835–1921)

"Marche royale du lion" [Royal March of the Lion] is the second selection from Saint-Saëns's *Le Carnaval des animaux.* It is the introductory movement of the suite and includes the fourth string notes. This melody was transposed for pedagogical considerations.

- Make sure to count out loud away from the guitar and while playing.
- Continue to sing note names out loud.
- Continue to consider left- and right-hand points.

Marche royale du lion

Tortues
From Le Carnaval des animaux
Camille Saint-Saëns (1835–1921)

"Tortues" [Tortoises] is the final selection from Saint-Saens's *Le Carnaval des animaux*. It includes the C note; in fact, the excerpt ends with a descending C scale. This example was also transposed for pedagogical considerations. Lastly, "Tortues" should be played at a slow tempo.

- Make sure to count out loud away from the guitar and while playing.
- Note the repeated i fingers that begin m. 1 and m. 4.
- Play at a slow tempo.
- Continue to sing note names out loud and consider technical points.

Tortues

Supplemental: Kleine Romanze
Robert Schumann (1810–1856)

“Kleine Romanze” [Little Romance] is the nineteenth movement in Schumann’s *Album for the Young*. In addition to including notes on the fourth string, it is also a good review for dotted quarter notes. The piece is also a right-hand challenge including many inverted string crosses.

- Make sure to count out loud away from the guitar and while playing.
- Note the many inverted crosses, including a few descending crosses.
- Continue to sing note names out loud and consider technical points.

Kleine Romanze

• ACCIDENTALS

Accidentals are indications that a pitch should be played one-half step higher or lower. This chapter will include key signatures as well as the three primary types of accidental notes: sharps, flats and natural notes.

Sharps

A sharp symbol (#) indicates that a note should be played one-half step (or one fret) higher than the main note that follows it. Example 1 below notates this exact point. Example 2 illustrates that when a sharp or other accidental is notated within a measure, this sharp symbol is also applied to the remaining beats of that measure.

Example 1

Example 2

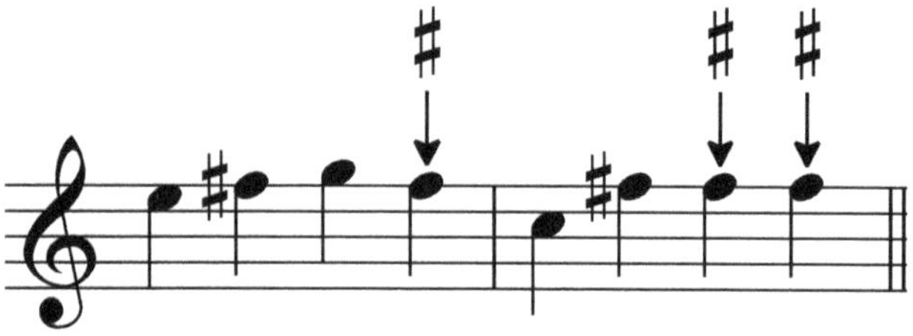

Rests

Notating rests has been described in the introduction of this method. The rests included in the remainder of Section II should be observed by allowing the appropriate finger to fall to the ringing string, thus dampening it.

Etude
op. 6, no. 11
Fernando Sor (1778-1839)

This is best-known as "Estudio 17," its title attributed by the great twentieth-century guitar virtuoso Andres Segovia. Segovia created his own edition of twenty selected Sor etudes. This excerpt contains the introductory melody.

- Make sure to observe the F#'s and quarter rests.
- Note the repeated i fingers between mm. 2-3 and mm. 4-5.
- Continue to count, sing note names out loud and consider technical points.

Etude

Supplemental: Trällerliedchen
From Album für die Jungend, op. 68
Robert Schumann (1810-1856)

"Trällerliedchen" [Little Humming Song] is the third piece in Robert Schuman's *Album for the Young*, op. 68, a set of forty-three short works that Schumann composed for his three daughters. Today, these works are highly regarded for their quality as artistic miniatures. More pieces from this cycle, as well as a similar one by Tchaikovsky, will be presented later in this section. This piece serves as an effective review of the concepts introduced so far as well. The A note in the last line was displaced by one octave for the purposes of this method.

- Note the repeated m fingers between phrases.
- Continue to sing note names out loud, count and consider technical points.

Make sure to count out loud away from the guitar and while playing, giving special consideration to the eighth notes.

Trällerliedchen

Flats

A flat symbol (b) indicates that a note should be played one fret lower than otherwise indicated. The below diagrams notate this exact point. Regarding the second diagram, the Bb will be used in the next piece while the Eb will be utilized in "Old French Folksong" and "Abschied."

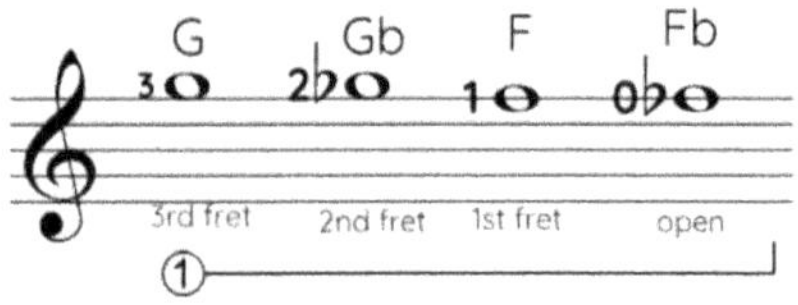

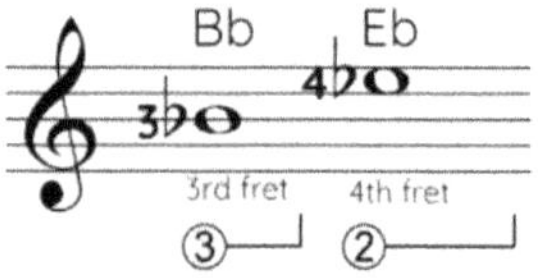

Bruder Martin
From Symphony no. 1, "Titan"
Gustav Mahler (1860–1911)

"Bruder Martin" [Frère Jacques] is a French folk song that composer Gustav Mahler incorporated in the third movement of his First Symphony ("Titan"). The melody below is the minor version that is utilized in Mahler's symphony.

- Remember to observe the Bb note on the third string.
- Note the repeated i fingers throughout the melody.
- Continue to sing note names out loud and consider technical points.

Bruder Martin

Supplemental: Old French Song
From Children's Album, op. 39
Piotr Tchaikovsky (1840–1893)

Piotr Tchaikovsky, inspired by Robert Schumann, composed his own set of twenty-four children's pieces and dedicated it to his nephew. This is the first of several selections from Tchaikovsky's work presented in this method.

- Remember to observe the Bb note on the third string, and Eb note on the second string.
- Observe right hand fingerings.
- Continue to sing note names out loud and consider technical points.

Old French Song

Key Signatures

A key signature indicates the tonal center or key of a piece. Each scale includes a unique profile of sharps, flats, and natural notes that is indicated at the beginning of the piece. Accidentals within a key signature apply to the entire piece. Key signatures utilized in this method are shown below.

C major/A minor

G major/E minor

D major/B minor

A major

D minor

Etude
op. 35, no. 22
Fernando Sor (1778–1839)

This etude is another selection from Segovia's collection of Sor etudes, where it is named Estudio 5. This excerpt includes the melody from the first section.

- Remember to play F# and C# because the melody is in the key of B minor.
- Note the E# in m. 7.
- Continue to sing note names out loud and consider technical points.

Etude

Supplemental: Pe loc
From Romanian Folk Dances
Sz. 56, BB. 68
Béla Bartók (1881–1945)

"In One Spot" or ("Pe loc") is the third of Béla Bartók's six *Romanian Folk Dances* composed for piano. Bartók later arranged the work for orchestra, as well as for several small ensembles, including violin and guitar.

In this arrangement, the time signature was changed from 2/4 to 4/4.

- Remember to play F# and C# because the melody is in the key of D major.
- Observe quarter and whole rests.
- Continue to sing note names out loud and consider technical points.

Pe loc

Sharps, Flats and Natural Notes

A natural note is not played as a sharp or flat regardless of the key signature. It in a sense neutralizes or overrides an accidental indicated by the key signature. See the example below.

Example 3

Abschied
From 6 Lieder, op. 89
Mauro Giuliani (1781–1829)

“Abschied” is a song for soprano and guitar composed by Italian composer Mauro Giuliani. The text is in German, and the piece is written in the style of Franz Schubert (1797–1828). The piece is in G major yet includes sharps, flats, and natural notes. It is the most rhythmically challenging selection presented thus far.

- Make sure to count out loud away from the guitar and while playing.
- Note the F natural in m. 7 and Eb in m. 9.
- Continue to sing note names out loud and consider technical points.

Abschied

Supplemental: Ave verum corpus
Excerpt from K. 618
Wolfgang Amadeus Mozart (1756–1791)

“Ave verum corpus” is a Eucharistic chant that has been set to music by many composers, most notably Wolfgang Amadeus Mozart (1756–1791) in his motet “Ave verum corpus,” K. 618, which is the version of the melody presented below.

- Note the key signature of D major.
- Note accidentals including sharps, flats, and natural notes.
- Observe rests and ties.
- Continue to sing note names out loud and consider technical points.

Ave verum corpus

• NOTES ON THE FIFTH STRING

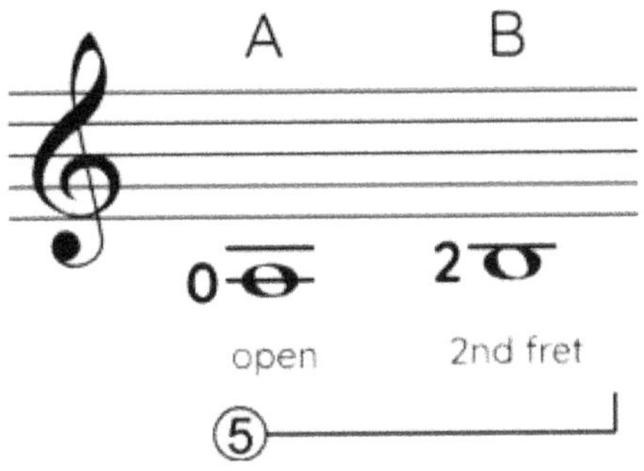

The A-minor scale includes the introduced notes on the fifth string. The thumb movement will be the same as that in the C-major scale.

A-Minor Scale

Wiegenlied
op. 49, no. 4
Johannes Brahms (1833–1897)

Johannes Brahms's "Wiegenlied" [Lullaby] is a song for voice and piano. The melody is also contained in the second movement of the composer's second symphony. The piece was transposed for pedagogical considerations.

- Be aware of the new notes contained below the staff on leger lines.
- Note the repeated m fingers throughout the melody.
- Continue to count, sing note names out loud and consider technical points.

Wiegenlied

Supplemental: Morning Prayer
From Children's Album, op. 39
Piotr Tchaikovsky (1840–1893)

"Morning Prayer" is the first movement of Tchaikovsky's miniature cycle for children, The *Children's Album*, op. 39.

- Remember to observe the C# and D# notes in the second line as well as the C natural and D natural notes in the third line.
- Be aware of the new notes included in the final line.
- Continue to count, sing note names out loud and consider technical points.

Morning Prayer

• NOTES ON THE SIXTH STRING

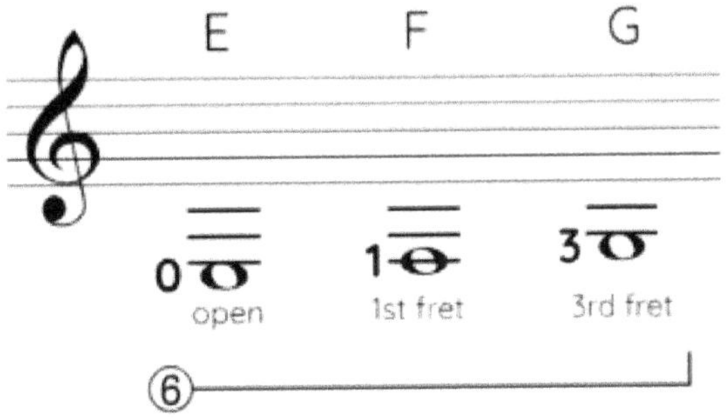

The following is the E-minor scale. Make sure to rest the thumb on the soundboard while playing the sixth string. The thumb movement for the remainder of the scale will be the same as the C-major and A-minor scales.

E-minor Scale

Playing Free strokes with the Thumb

The thumb functions the same way as the fingers.

1. Place the thumb on one of the lower strings pointed in and placed on the left corner of the nail. Rest the fingers on the top three strings.

2. Push into the string and play from the knuckle joint. Your finger should clear the next highest string. Note the follow-through of the thumb should not go inside the hand but rather over the fingers.

3. Let the thumb fall to the string and repeat the previous steps.

Thumb Exercise 1

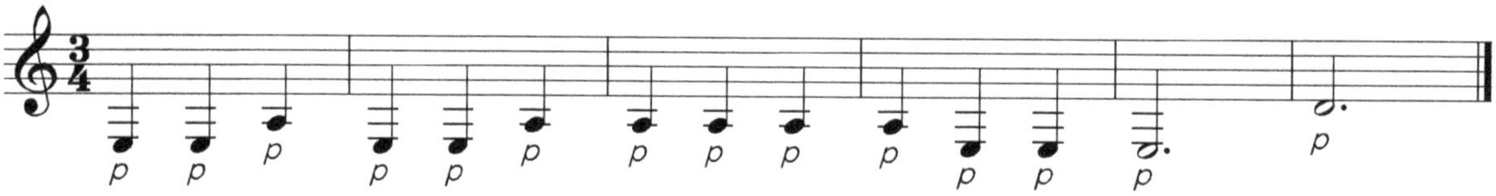

Malagueña
Traditional Spanish

"Malagueña" was composed by Cuban composer Ernesto Lecuona. "Malagueña" became so popular that many artists have created their own renditions. Although it was Lecuona's piece that popularized the tune, the melody itself was based on a folkloric Spanish tune.

- Play the selection with thumb strokes throughout.
- Note the G#'s throughout and G naturals in m. 4 and m. 12.
- Continue to count, sing note names out loud and consider technical points.

Malagueña

Supplemental: In Church
From Children's Album, op. 39
Piotr Tchaikovsky (1840–1893)

"In Church" is the penultimate movement of Tchaikovsky's *Children's Album*. The latter half of the piece includes a descending E-minor scale, which has been transposed down an octave for the purpose of this method.

- Note that the piece is in 2/4 which means each measures has two beats.
- Observe the newly introduced notes on the sixth string.
- Continue to sing note names out loud and consider technical points.

In Church

Section III:

Introductory Guitar Solos

While the first two sections of this method have introduced basic technique and reading skills, this section will introduce solo guitar playing as well as varying techniques to play multiple voices. In addition to being pedagogically sequenced, the solos have also been selected for their musical quality and stylistic diversity. The notation is largely what was preserved by the composer unless indicated otherwise. Each chapter of this section will introduce the new skills before introducing each piece.

• ALTERNATING THE THUMB AND FINGERS

The following exercise introduces the alternation of p with the i and m fingers. The top line (i and m) should be played with rest strokes while the bottom line (p) with free strokes. The exercise can be played with the following steps.

1. p plays, i falls to the first string.
2. i plays and rests on the second string, p falls to the sixth string.
3. p plays, m falls to the first string.
4. m plays and rests on the second string, i returns, p falls to the sixth string.
5. Repeat steps 1-4.

P-IM Alternating Exercise 1

Memorization

Solo guitar music is normally played from memory. The ability to memorize complex music is a skill that can be systematically developed. Memorizing music during the initial learning stages helps solidify memory and build confidence for performance. While learning the pieces in this section, begin by completing the following steps during each practice session while memorizing.

1. Count the rhythm of each voice of the first measure separately, then together.
2. Sing the note names of each voice.

3. Play the first measure with awareness of the proper right- and left-hand techniques.
4. Play the first measure while counting, then while singing the note names of each voice.
5. Play the first measure from memory.
6. Repeat steps 1–5 for the second measure.
7. Play the first two measures from memory.
8. Repeat steps 1–5 for the third measure.
9. Play the second two measures from memory.
10. Play all three measures from memory.
11. Continue in this manner, although do not go back any more than three measures (as in steps 7 and 9) before testing your memory from the beginning to the most recently memorized measure.

At the beginning of the next practice session, play the piece from memory. Begin the above process at the measure where the memory begins to slip. If you find that you have retained 50% of what you have learned the day before, do not worry; this is typical. Repeat this process daily until the entire piece is memorized. You will find that as you continue in this process your memory will improve and as a result your playing will become more confident. All the pieces moving forward should be memorized.

Malagueña
Traditional Spanish
Arr. Francesco Barone

The first guitar solo presented includes the same bass melody that was introduced in the last chapter; an upper accompanying E pedal is also included here.

- Play the upper pedal with rest strokes, once comfortable try with free strokes.
- Play the bottom line with free strokes.
- Use the instructions above to memorize the piece.

- Continue to count, sing note names out loud and consider technical points.

Malagueña

The following exercise will build upon the technique introduced in the first alternate p–im exercise. It should also be played with rest strokes in the top voice and free strokes in the bottom. Consider the following while practicing:

- When a thumb stroke follows, the finger that just played should remain rested on the next lowest string to provide support for the thumb stroke.
- The thumb should rest on the strings indicates with an x note head.
- The fingers should otherwise function as if they were alternating without the thumb.

P-IM Alternating Exercise 2

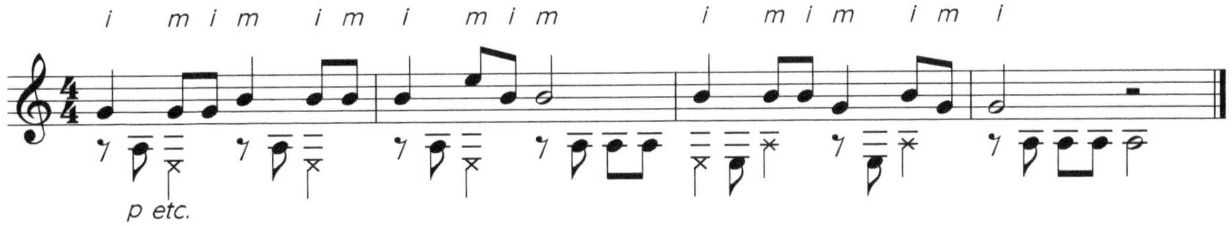

Second Position

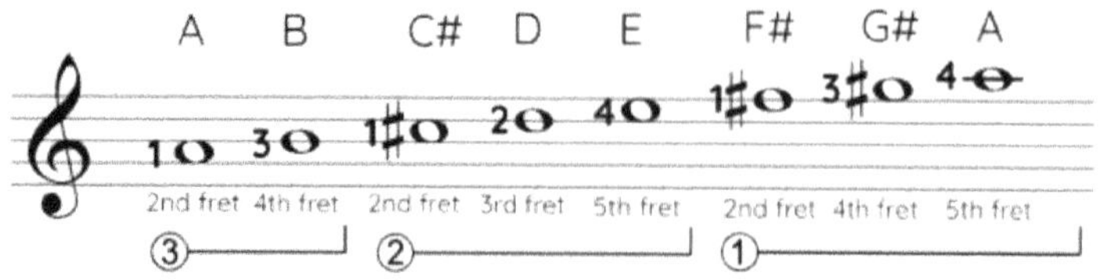

A-major Scale

Dotted Eighth Notes

Before discussing dotted eight notes, sixteenth notes need to be introduced. A sixteenth note (note with two flags) divides the beat in to four parts and is counted 1 e & a. The dotted eighth note sustains for three quarters of a beat (one eighth note plus one sixteenth note). The exercises below will introduce dotted eighth notes and sixteenth notes.

Rhythmic Exercise 10

Rhythmic Exercise 11

Long, Long Ago
Thomas Haynes Bayly (1737–1839)
Arr. Francesco Barone

"Long, Long Ago," composed by English poet and songwriter Thomas Haynes Bayly, was a popular song of the 1840s. It was first composed as a vocal piece with orchestral accompaniment. More recently it has become a staple in the Suzuki violin and guitar repertoires. My arrangement has preserved the introduction as well as the melody from the 1913 recorded version.

- Play the melody with rest strokes, once comfortable try with free strokes.
- Remember to observe the key signature of A Major by playing F#s, C#s, and G#s.
- Memorize the piece using the method described in the last section.

Long, Long Ago

• PLAYING THE THUMB AND FINGERS TOGETHER

The following exercise serves as a preparation for playing the thumb and fingers together.

P-IM Alternation Exercise 3

The Barre

The barre is a left-hand technique in which the first finger is laid across a fret to sustain multiple notes. There are two things to consider when forming a barre: 1) using the weight of the arm to sustain the barre and 2) being selective in barre placement.

When holding a barre, it is critical to leverage the weight of the arm rather than clamping with pressure from the hand; doing so will produce the clearest sound with minimum effort. Regarding barre placement, the finger should be placed slightly on the left side.

To practice the barre, play m. 2 of Thema as an excerpt. For this practice spot lay the barre across the top four strings.

Thema
From Variations sur les "Folies D'Espagne," op. 45
Mauro Giuliani (1781-1829)

Giuliani's "Abshied" was presented earlier in this volume. This selection is the theme from Giuliani's variations on la Folia, or a standard melody line and stock chord progression used in compositions since the 1500's.

- Play both lines with free strokes.
- Take note of the barre technique in m. 2 and m. 10.
- Memorize the piece.

Thema

• BASS - CHORD PLAYING

The next two exercises should be practiced with free strokes.

This is the first exercise in which the a finger is utilized. The a finger will function the same way as the i and m fingers. Make sure to push into the string and move from the knuckle joint as you would with the i and m fingers.

1. The thumb should begin on the sixth string, the fingers should be placed on the top three strings (i finger on the third string, m finger on the second string, and a finger on the first string) with the knuckle joints over their corresponding fingers.
2. Move the fingers from the knuckle joints into the hand.
3. The thumb plays, the fingers fall to their corresponding strings.
4. The fingers play, the thumb falls to the sixth string. The fingers should stay in the hand just as they were in step 2.
5. Steps 3 & 4 repeat.

Bass-Chord Exercise 1

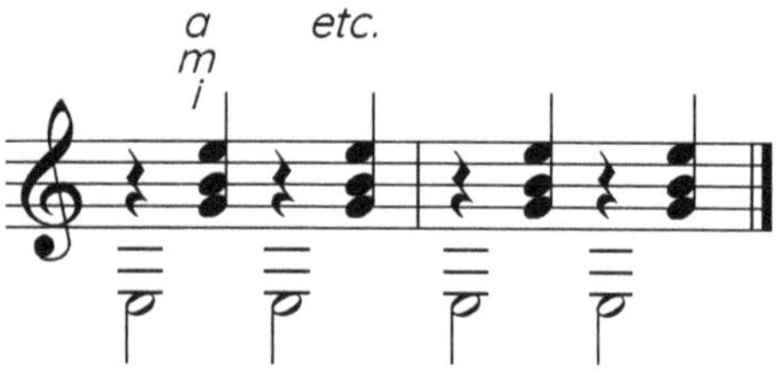

Bass-Chord Exercise 2

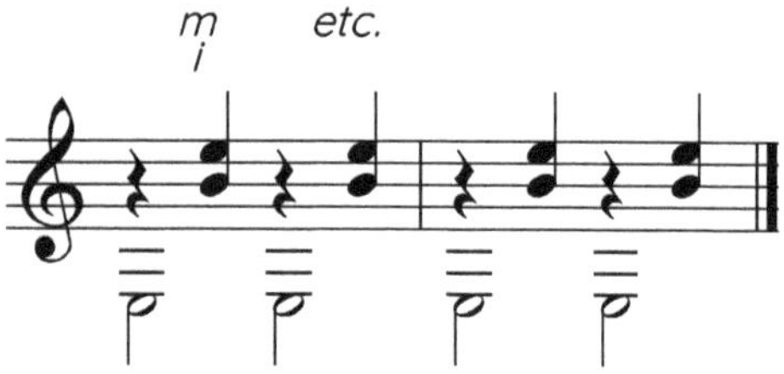

The following exercise will prepare the student to play the final passage of Lesson 61 (see below). Note that the i and a fingers should be planted in m. 5 in the same way they are in m. 1 and m. 3.

1. m.1 (also mm. 3 and 5): The thumb plays bass C, the i and a fingers fall to the G and E notes.
2. m. 1-2 (also mm. 3–4): The i and a fingers play, the p and m finger fall to the fourth and second strings.
3. m. 5: The same as step 2, except i and a will be played separately.

Preparation Exercise

Lesson 61
Julio Segreras (1879–1942)

Julio Segreras was an Argentine guitarist who is best known for his six-volume method. This piece, titled "Lesson 61," is contained in the first volume of the guitarist's method. The piece is also included in the third volume of the Suzuki Guitar Method although renamed (by Suzuki Guitar pioneer Frank Longay) "Calliope."

"Lesson 61" is an introductory piece for the thumb/fingers technique presented. The final measures depart from the technique being studied; therefore, I would work on the preparation exercise above before memorizing the rest of the piece.

- Play free strokes with bass-chord technique.
- Work on the final two measures before learning the remainder of the piece.
- Memorize the piece.

Lesson 61

• PLUCKED CHORDS

The following exercises should be practiced with free strokes.

1. The fingers should begin by resting on the following strings: p on the sixth string, i finger on the third string, m finger on the second string, and a finger on the first string for the first exercise). The knuckle joints should be over their corresponding strings.
2. Pluck the thumb and fingers simultaneously. Allow the thumb and fingers return to their original position over the string.
3. Allow the thumb and fingers to fall to their corresponding strings.
4. Repeat steps 2 and 3.

Plucked Chord Exercise 1

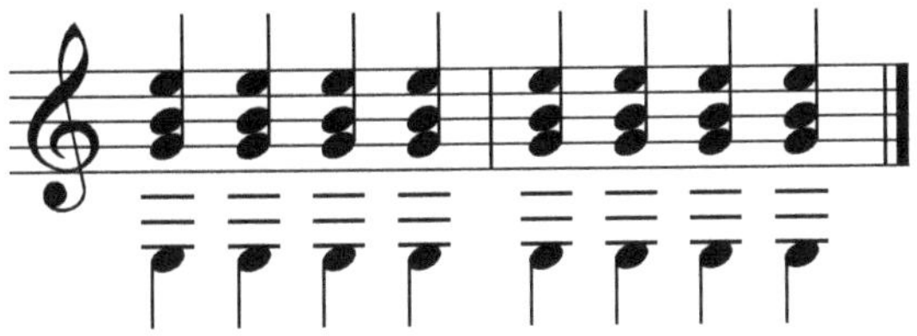

Plucked Chord Exercise 2

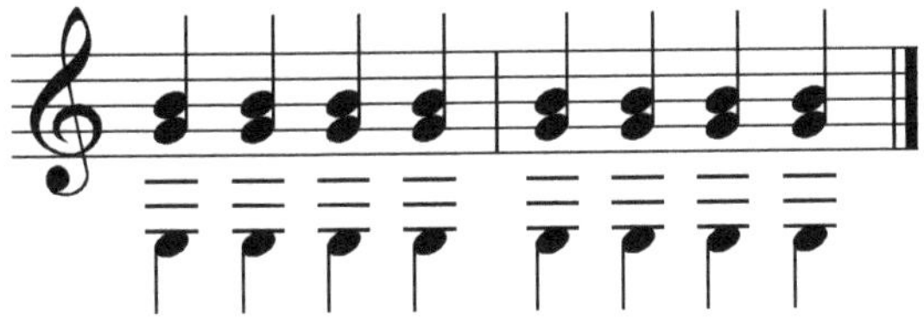

Chord Progressions

The chord voicings below are found in the theme and variations that follow. These progressions are common to many styles of music and are labeled with roman numerals.

I-ii-V7-I in C

I-ii-V-I in C

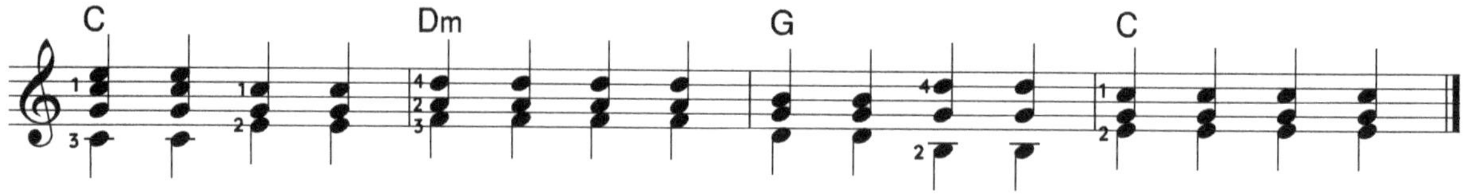

I-IV-V-I in G

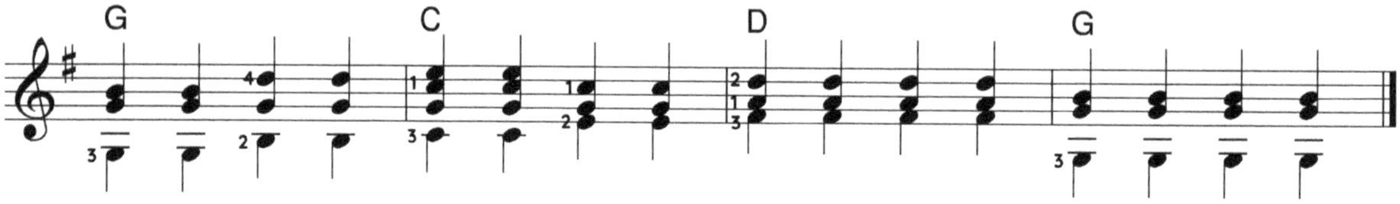

vii°-I in E

Theme
From 10 Variations for Guitar op. 16
Joseph Küffner (1776–1856)

Joseph Küffner worked as a violinist for the Würzburg court orchestra and as bandmaster of the Bavarian Army regiment. As a composer, he was known for contributing to the solo and chamber guitar repertory. The theme that follows is part of Küffner's *10 Variations for Guitar,* op. 16.

This theme provides a valuable introduction to plucked chords. It also conveys harmonic interest without left hand formations that are overly challenging for this level. Küffner includes several expressive indices within the piece. These include the following:

- Dynamic indications: *piano* (p), an indication to play softly; *mezzo forte* (mF), a medium dynamic; and *fortissimo* (FF), an indication to play very loudly.
- Expressive indications: *con expressione,* to play with expression or feeling; *calando,* to gradually decrease in volume; *cres(cendo),* to gradually increase in volume.
- Accent (>): an indication to place emphasis on a note or chord.

A final note, all of the right- and left-hand fingerings have been added by the author since the original manuscript does not include fingerings. The fingerings used in the preceding chord exercises should be utilized in this piece whenever possible. Alternate fingerings are included in the end notes as well as the original phrase markings. Although an explanation for the editorial decision of the latter cannot be covered within the scope of this book, the removal of the markings will not affect the way the edited passages will be played.

Be aware of the following points while playing.

- Play the piece with plucked chords, always playing the bottom note with the thumb.
- Use the left-hand fingerings presented in the preceding chord exercises.
- Observe the dynamic indications and bar line repeats.
- Memorize the piece.

Theme

Editorial Notes:

Theme

mm. 2, 6, & 15. Original:

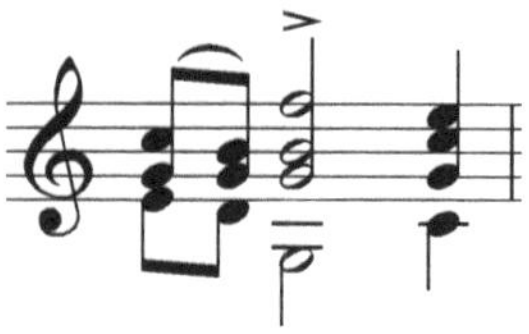

m. 3. Original:

m. 3. Alternate Fingering:

m. 4. Original:

mm. 8 & 17. Original:

mm. 8 & 17: Alternate Fingering:

m. 12. Alternate Fingering:

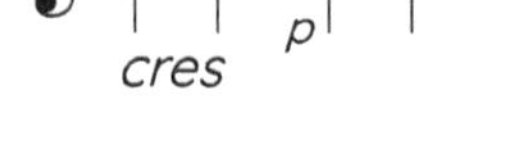

Suggested Resources for Further Study

Below, I have included resources that I think will a helpful next step beyond this book. I have listed everything by topic for the convenience of the reader. Those resources useful for multiple categories have been listed multiple times.

Arpeggios

Brouwer, Leo. *Œuvres pour guitar/Guitar Works I (Guitar Solo)*. Paris: Editions Durand, 2006.

Provost, Richard. *Classical Guitar Technique, vol. 2: Developing Arpeggio Technique*. West Hartford, CT: Professional Guitar Publications, 1985; 2nd ed., 1992; 3rd rev. edition San Francisco: Guitar Solo, 2007.

Barres

Tennant, Scott, and Nathaniel Gunod. *Complete Pumping Nylon: The Classical Guitarist's Technique Handbook*. Van Nuys, CA: Alfred Music, 2016.

Chords

Barone, Francesco. *Guitar Chords in Context: A Beginner Guitar Chord Method for Kids and Adults*. Medford, MA: Barone, 2020.

Berle, Arnie. *Chords & Progressions for Jazz & Popular Guitar*. New York: Amsco Publications, 1992.

Memorization/ Practice Skills

Kaplan, Burton. *Practicing for Artistic Success: The Musician's Guide to Self-Empowerment*. Morris, NY: Perception Development Techniques, 2004.

Provost, Richard. *The Art & Technique of Practice*. San Francisco: Guitar Solo, 1992.

Nails

Tennant, Scott. *Complete Pumping Nylon: The Classical Guitarist's Technique Handbook*. Van Nuys, CA: Alfred Music, 2016.

Reading

Berle, Arnie. *New Guitar Techniques for Sight-Reading*. Van Nuys, CA: Alfred Music, 1991.

Noad, Frederick M. *Solo Guitar Playing, vol. 1.* New York: Schirmer Books, 1994.

Scales

Provost, Richard. *Classical Guitar Technique, vol. 1: Scale Source Book.* West Hartford, CT: Professional Guitar Publications, 1983; 2nd ed., 1992; 3rd rev. edition San Francisco: Guitar Solo, 2002.

Tennant, Scott. *Complete Pumping Nylon: The Classical Guitarist's Technique Handbook.* Van Nuys, CA: Alfred Music, 2016.

About the Author

Classical Guitarist Francesco Barone has graced stages across the United States as both a soloist and chamber musician. He has been prominently featured by esteemed guitar festivals and societies, including the Boston Classical Guitar Society, New England Guitar Society, Connecticut Guitar Society, and The Hartt School Guitar Festival. A prize-winner of the Philadelphia Classical Guitar Society Guitar Competition, his performances have also been broadcast on NPR.

Beyond traditional concert settings, Barone actively engages with local communities, regularly performing outreach concerts at town libraries throughout New England. He connects with younger audiences by performing house concerts nationwide through the classical music startup Groupmuse. His highly anticipated debut album, which includes works by Bach, Giuliani, Martin, and Koshkin, is slated for release in late 2025.

As a dedicated educator, Barone has authored two innovative guitar methods. "Guitar Chords in Context" employs pedagogical sequencing for mastering guitar chords, while "Beginning Classical Guitar" integrates the Suzuki Method, traditional techniques, and the teachings of his late mentor, Richard Provost, into a cohesive approach to classical guitar education. Barone has taught at The Hartt School of Music, Columbia University, and CT State College. He currently serves as a lecturer in guitar and music theory at Saint Anselm College and as the Suzuki Program Director at Wayland School of Music.

Barone holds a Doctorate of Musical Arts and a Master of Music from The Hartt School, University of Hartford. Originally from the Philadelphia area, he earned his Bachelor of Music from Temple University. He performs on a 2018 Alan Chapman guitar.

Before you close this book...

...and place it on the bookshelf.

Before you retire this read...

...and move on.

Please consider leaving a review.

Your review will help readers find Beginning Classical Guitar!

Amazon uses everything from the review quantity, star rating, recency, keywords, and sentiment to sort and rank listed products.

But that's not all...

Your review will also help me create content tailored to you!

I look back at customer reviews and feedback to come up with ideas for new method books.

I also use your feedback to edit and improve upon my published works.

So please consider leaving a review so I can better serve you as well as future readers.

Review Now.

https://amzn.to/47bK5rr

www.ingramcontent.com/pod-product-compliance
Ingram Content Group UK Ltd.
Pitfield, Milton Keynes, MK11 3LW, UK
UKHW051118290926
15471UKWH00010B/1746

9 798993 304205